HOW TO LEAVE YOUR FAMILY

poems by

Maeve Holler

Finishing Line Press
Georgetown, Kentucky

HOW TO LEAVE
YOUR FAMILY

Copyright © 2024 by Maeve Holler
ISBN 979-8-88838-466-4 First Edition
All rights reserved under International and Pan-American Copyright Conventions. No part of this book may be reproduced in any manner whatsoever without written permission from the publisher, except in the case of brief quotations embodied in critical articles and reviews.

Publisher: Leah Huete de Maines
Editor: Christen Kincaid
Cover Art: Eli Pillaert
Author Photo: Maeve Holler
Cover Design: Maeve Holler

Order online: www.finishinglinepress.com
also available on amazon.com

Author inquiries and mail orders:
Finishing Line Press
PO Box 1626
Georgetown, Kentucky 40324
USA

Contents

Family Tree ix

PROLOGUE
Into The Night, I Try xii

GRAFTING TUPELO
The Art of It All 1
Talking Blossoms 2
Ivy Curse 3
Funeral 4
The Secret Matrimony of Control & Desire 5
Magnolia 6
Symptom 7
How to Leave Your Family 9
The Twilight Man 10
Tupelo Granny Waitresses 11
You Are Giving Me Some Other Love 12
If I Never See the Setting Sun Again 13

AN ONLY MOON
Shades of Pink 17
Method Acting 18
Homecoming 19
Make Do 20
Half Stitch 21
In Orbit 22
An Only Moon 23
Boogie Down, St. Rose 24
Tupelo Granny, Paper Doll Hot Mess 25
Who Needs to Pray? 27

IVY MATH
I Was Born 31
Small Angry Mama 32
The Goodness 33
When I Was Four 34

Our Music 35
Lucky 36
I Can Still Hear the Nights We Dream 38
Tupelo Granny Sleeps, Wishbone Poppy Wakes 39
I'm In Florida With You 41
Belated Elegy: Moth, Flame 42
Six Ways to Play Possum 43
H-A-Y-T 44
White Noise 45
Wishbone Poppy 46

VALLEY BLUE
She Chants at My Sleeping Body 51
Stewing 52
Lilies of the Valley 54
On Becoming Woman 55
Blue Math 56
Cannibal Flower 57
In The Valley Raintime, I Am 59
The Hole Where My Door Once Was 60
Walmart and Other Valley Hangouts 61
10 Minutes of Blue 62
I Still Smell You, Distance Aside 63
In Which I Finally Say Thank You 66
To My Granny 67
Locust Bride 68
I'm Getting There 69
The Dirt Which Births Us 70
Otherlife 71

EPILOGUE
A Point of Balance Between Two Stars 75

Acknowledgments 76
Notes 77

FAMILY TREE

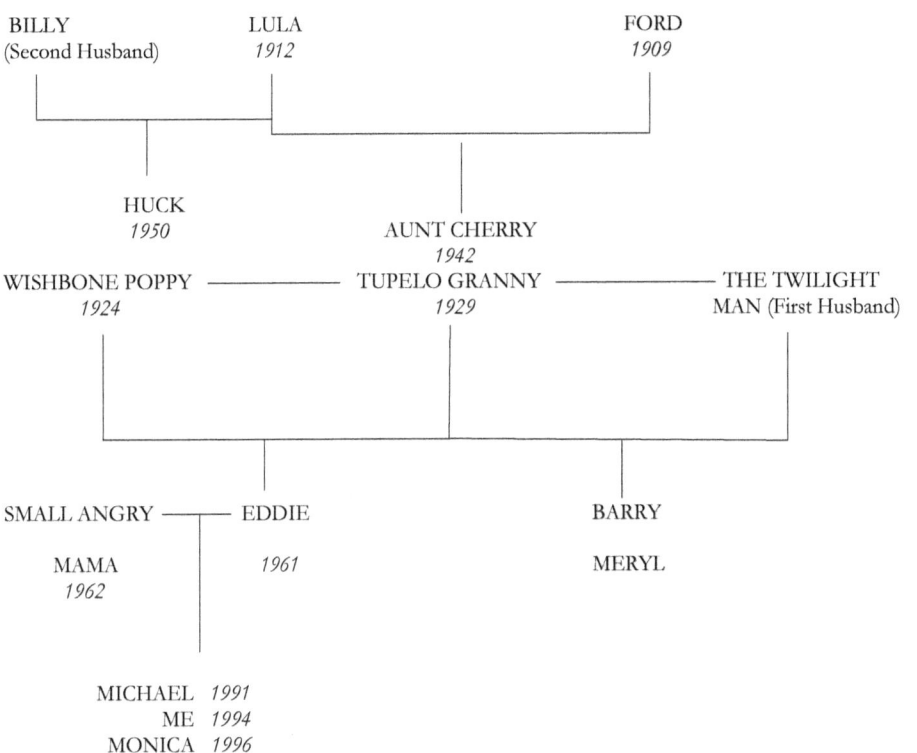

ix

PROLOGUE

INTO THE NIGHT, I TRY

For My Granny, 1929 - 2002

I swear, I tried hard to cry, to summon myself backward
in the shape of grief. I lie in bed, my dry eyes shut tight,

calling back flashes of your image, fighting calculations
of missed opportunity, attempting desperately to retrace

the complex map of a now-irretrievable place. I tried,
at your funeral, to understand how large, marble slabs

sculpted into busts of Catholic saints, stained glass windows,
cheap shiraz & endless trays packed with Penne Ala Vodka

could ever honor the laurels you crafted in this dimension.
I *tried* to channel you, in that empty bathroom at your wake

in Bayonne, my voice sputtering out onto the seafoam tile
like a dying car battery, whining low with electric fatigue.

I tried to sketch the division between the loss of *you* & you,
as in you, the body, and you, a soul swimming in a new timeline.

You couldn't hear me then, but I tried, like I'm trying now—
to stockpile the tokens of your being, to salvage voice,

to poem & poem & poem in your name until I hollow out
some tiny, mangled inlet for your effigy to navigate,

until the *you* stuck between the transmission of two realities
can gutter my tunnel of language. I want you to hitchhike

these words like escape, like they're gushing toward Georgia
and you can't sit still because Meryl & Barry aren't by your side.

I want you to drag race & shot gun & hotwire your way out
til the stars collectivize and project your ghost in protest

of the hand you were dealt. I *need* the earth shook & moonstruck,
bathing long in your down-home-up-do-beauty-queen ways.

I'm riddled with finding the best vehicle for your phantom ride,
& sometimes I'm worried you're stuck in that purgatorial plane

shouting Mississippi epithets toward the flimsy ground I stand on,
as if to warn me, to say *stay away*. To go dark & take it all back.

But I keep on scribbling heaping tributes to your mortal likeness
in the morning light: aubades for confidence, for ruthlessness,

for the keyed-up little girl from Tupelo helming a faulty, vacant ship
into a sea that was never meant to be discovered. Granny, I know

you never asked me to do this, but you warrant a love story.
So, I'm writing it: I want the world offended when you slowly sway

your hips across the page. I want it hurt by your foul bayonet tongue,
slashing up & down this unfit canvas like you invented blasphemy.

I want the world to see you wife disaster in flocks of lilac—I want it
embarrassed & cuckolded & smitten with your grit. I swear, it'll fall

head over heels, sending dried red roses by the dozen, doting notes
enclosed. You are the mother of the talking blossoms I call family

& when vertigo raided your brain, my 7-year-old-self ate the fruit
of attempt. I *tried* to cry, I *tried* to exorcize the stroke from your body,

spouting all the Our Fathers & Hail Marys & broken Apostle's Creeds
I could muster until I realized that not even God could change you back.

I tried to peek under the skirt of your story, and I'll keep trying
until you bend back some bastard refraction of light & whisper

that it's *okay* to just breathe now. That you're ready for the silence:
for the exercise in dispossession to come full stop & to embrace

the grip of endless night.

GRAFTING TUPELO

"I have several people inside me,
all gathering a force I've never seen and all
strung like paper dolls across the window
that opens in a half-moon and portrays itself
loving the world in a seldom-seen rocket
coming at the girl who is most visible, most
reliable, in spring—when the world slips
into treble, all the time itching about life
and ignoring the thing we call death."

—*Maureen Seaton, "Year of the Carousel Horses"*

THE ART OF IT ALL

Tupelo, Mississippi, February 1929

When Annie was born, she talked in blossoms.
Lula and Ford made sure Tupelo was grafted onto her skin
like a scattered blue map, so she sang the Ivy chorus all night long.
While her family went buck wild for whiskey cokes & naked lady games,
she splashed in the art of it all. She played, just like she thought a child should,
with shadow men & paper dolls. Of course, she wasn't always Tupelo Granny.
Before that, Annie was delicate. She was doily. She was blush. She scribed
the harsh beauty of her small planet like the mother of all that is green.
But, even from her birth, she conjured up a different lung. Annie held
the family curse in her belly like sin, as if *she* was to blame
for the thunder which plagued her people. This was the mass
she carried around. And, cancerous or not, it always felt like a tornado
inside of her—a spinning stiletto force, pulling her weight
relentlessly in the direction of ruin.

TALKING BLOSSOMS

Tupelo, Mississippi, 1936

Tupelo Granny's baby bed is ripped from her sodden home while she slumbers. Her dreams cling like molasses to the mattress as her gaunt body spins in the windwaves like some ragdoll, a throwaway. She sees it all up there, in the heaven sky—the milk truck, cow flesh, whole houses, all spinning & hell bound.

In the tornado, she becomes one with the world. A skeletal sacrifice for the gum pond. With force, a blue steel nail cradles itself in her chest, and with each gust of earth spray, it drives itself tighter into the cavern which holds her heart. When she returns to the ground, she's still just a girl—she seeps for salvation, for the dawn sky.

*

Tupelo Granny sighs in the calm, still in her pale-yellow Easter dress. This is the waiting game. Tornado afterlife. Her body pinned against a tree, spidery legs loose in the stormwater. She watches while the foggy sea beneath swallows plump satsumas, ripe from above. In this inverted world, Tupelo Granny thinks of the chickens, their wet uselessness, her second cousin Robert & his pink, empty gums growing a third set of teeth. Tonguing her loose, cracked & yellowed fangs, she sucks an old molar out of its misery, holding it in her fist like a talisman, praying to be undone.

*

With the wreck, her daddy's bones blew out, some family passed, but eventually, she learned to become less injured in the hushlight. Her body, her home—reclaimed by the earth as talking blossoms. And in death, she was born again, returned to the storm & scattered like dirt. We now pray on Easter Sunday to the heaven sky finality. It's warm to play back her rotting, smoked voice:

Honey, don't pull out them baby teeth—if ya do, you'll grow a third set in ya 20's.

IVY CURSE

    Memphis, Tennessee, 1942

The tornado had its way with Ford—
it hurt him in places only Lula had seen until that day.

When it leveled his home & tore his back all haywire,
he went 4F. He sat futile on the world's sidelines,

watching the war like a drunken backseat driver.
Since he was one of those *good* Mississippi boys,

loyalty tore like blame through his mind,
so he scored a job in a defense plant & herded

the family off to Memphis. Ford worked
in the netherworld factory piecing together

ammunition & RDX as if it was his civic duty—as if
it was the least he could do. When the plant's

high voltage motor went bunk, he flared to its rescue
& gave the old thing his best shot. But the motor loved him

in the same jagged way the tornado had. The electricity
surged through Ford's heart like stormwater,

opaque & dirty with yesterday. The workers in the factory
all yelled in lakes for his body to kick back:

FORD FORD CAN YOU HEAR ME FORD
but he had already sputtered out into black nightshade.

Maybe he died so quick because of his sweaty skin,
or because the way his blood swelled thick

under the current's pressure. Either way, Ford
had it coming. He was an Ivy, and that was reason enough.

The other workers carried on, crafting tools for combat.
It was like nothing happened. He lay there still, laced

by rainbow wires growing around him in vines,
playing patriot in the best way he could.

FUNERAL

Tupelo, Mississippi, 1943

Ford climbed the sky & his old life on the ground hued chaotic—
the Ivy women bent back toward Mississippi, hunting afterlife,
& Tupelo Granny stood bull-headed against the inevitable twisting.
Lula billowed with loss, crossbrained & speeding toward vice,

as if she knew the rain would never pass. Her body took a new form:
the weak lioness, tearing her womb bloody. She disappeared
to Alabama & Tupelo Granny made a home in the still water.
An heir to her daddy's misfortune, she took a new job & got hitched

to the Twilight Man. She didn't know much about him,
but he was a man with cash. He loved her youth. Her desperation.
And like two mosquitos, they bred in that muddy puddle,
giving curse to two new lives. She raised up her baby sister,

and when Cherry was soon grown, she'd whisper blue metaphor
in the meat of night: *this storm isn't just yours or mine. It's ours, Annie,*
& they carried it in the best way they knew how: scabs picked,
skin worn thin, arms outstretched, grasping at the sky.

THE SECRET MATRIMONY OF CONTROL & DESIRE

Tupelo, Mississippi, 1944

*

The first few months were lemon puckered & honey plaid. Tupelo Granny was a broke down Chevy pickup & he climbed in her rusty flatbed like a horsefly to candied plums. It was summer and the Mississippi air had a way of making even the keenest folk fall stupid to love. She had it *all*—the A-lines, gingham crisp, high cheeks, fat skirts. And she thought he was a fine man, especially when she flashed a mirror toward her sunless past. She was 14 years old. She had no money, no home. They married in the backyard. It was hurried, unwell bliss by no other name.

*

The shiners came before her first child was even born: home from work, he'd fire walk & drag her back over hot coals. He kept her jobless & beehived & still she sang *yes, honey, no, baby* like a boxer haggling a cage match. Like it was God who taught her the language of submission. The Twilight Man stung her pockmarked until she swelled up, until her pregnant body, sanded to the coop like livestock mooned in squawks over the impossibility of flight.

*

Two babies later, Tupelo Granny became part of the forest. Her body had stopped craving escape. She meshed with the evergreens & thorny brush, her blood running through the woodland, trying only to lose herself along the blended pathways. But she, the forest, an intricate labyrinth, simply existed as a vestibule for the Twilight Man's latest shape of hurt. He slashed her thicket, pulled up her roots like weeds, flattened her habitat into a vulgar abyss. And Tupelo Granny, a mother all the same, just folded herself deeper into that green, the veins of her leaves swollen with cacophony.

MAGNOLIA

In the murder night
yowls of poultry
sober the lush air—

headless, coral sap
splatters their herded feathers
later plucked, done up,

set for sale. You see,
this landscape seeps turbulent.
Proud men make ragdolls

of whatever runs:
wives, workers, their watery
bodies flung to feed

the sore crimson soil.
They say, that's just how it is
in these parts. The rain

gotta come *somehow.*
And even the sodden ones
play the fell charade:

A rusty shotgun
in hand mimics the power
used to flatten blades

of weak pasture grass.
And, once you find that needle
in the hay, you believe.

You believe it when
they ask, *wasn't it God who
burnt our tongues at dusk?*

*Wasn't it He who
pulled our teeth, made us wrangle
in the dirt for blood?*

SYMPTOM

In the pale foil of slumber,
        Tupelo Granny turns

to face the moon's gaping eye.
        It focuses & flares down on her—

a spy to her spiraling eclipse.
        Lying next to the Twilight Man,

the eye only throbs toward her,
        lapping sleep from her ballooning

heart. Her eyelids are stonefed
        in the skylight: ruins of a fuller

anterior self. The eye whispers:
        Is this a dense death of gravity?

Is your body only the gathering
        of a thousand glimmering pinhole

projections? Is there a camera
        hidden in the moon? Her skin

bulges as the particles of her body
        to unravel and melt

into dreamscape. Her swarming
        mass pours out the window,

taking the shape of Selene.
        She is the target of this sick

awakening. Outside of herself,
        she will own a plot of the galaxy

& make hushed vortex love
        with constellations. They'll kiss

in antimatter, in secret canary
        bursts of momentum.

And, if worship exists
        in the ulterior world,

she will be the pulsing
        center of it all—she,

a symptom of fire,
        a fragmented corpse,

a starcrossed refugee churning
        the memory of rebirth.

HOW TO LEAVE YOUR FAMILY

Tupelo, Mississippi, 1947

Plot his movements for months. Know when he comes, goes, sleeps, smokes, eats, drinks, shits. Chart all of this and narrow down a gap: the 13 minutes in the middle of the night where you might be able to get away. Practice slipping out of his grasp in bed without waking him. Memorize the map for Interstate 20. Pack no bags, cause no suspicion. Save any pennies leftover from grocery runs. Buy extra diapers and store them in the trunk under the spare tire. Pick a place to hide—a city big enough that anonymity is possible. One close enough so you won't run out of gas. Research Atlanta's women's shelters at the library. Train the babies not to cry when you pluck them from their slumber. Train them to not ask questions. To let go.

On the chosen night, bestow a 6-pack and a bottle upon him. Cook his favorite cornbread and skirt steak. Make him happy. Make him love you in his ugly, gluttonous way. Eat plenty for your final meal. Once he's drunk in front of the TV, sneak a change of clothes & coat into the car, your shoes next to the door. Dress in your nightgown, slide into bed, and kiss him goodnight. Close your eyes and play possum. Run the plan through your head for the next four & a half hours. Hear him snore. Hear him fall in and out of dream state. Hear him almost awake. Hear his breath rise & sink. Hear his heartbeat in the final moments. Slip out of his gridlock. Do not breathe. Gather the babies, carefully placing your hands over their mouths. Shoes on, keys in hand, out the front door. Fasten the babies in their seats. Do not breathe. Get in. Get ready. Do not breathe. Start the engine. With the headlights off, pull out carefully, slowly. Pull down the block. Lights on. Do not breathe. Begin to cry. To feel relief.

Hear a man's voice. Look in the rearview mirror. See him running down the block with a shotgun. Feel your belly go ice box. Inside out. Get dragged back home. Get ragdolled. Get dumb bitch'ed. Get soaked red. Skin yellowed. Welted. Let him fall back asleep. Rage in prayer. Start plotting again. And again. Let him drag you back and beat you into blind surrender. Repeat until you operate on malfunction. Until you realize he's only after the kids. Until you become numb enough to leave your own blood behind. Promise yourself you'll be back for them. Know the forest can only be so thick. Repeat. Do not breathe. Do not cry. Drive. Drive. Drive. Do not think. Do not stop. Do not breathe. Just drive.

THE TWILIGHT MAN

Atlanta, Georgia, 1947

visits Tupelo Granny in the vertebrae of her dreams.
Out of terror particles, his body materializes like fiction,

chants INCUBUS in threes. She is lucid when he trances,
her chest a transistor channel singing his hollow pounding.

She listens deep, pinpointing the radio pulsing inside of her.
The Twilight Man's staccato sketches lo-fi over the static,

calling out ANN—ANN, IS THAT YOU? and the sound echoes
shrill over the course of her intestines. She is animal again,

running howls of adrenaline like a coyote in the witching hour.
Tupelo Granny prays in ethereal, packs a bag, drafting a plan

to go fugitive in the maps of possibility underneath the earth.
In the dirt there's no satellite, no poles, no echolocation, she knows.

But still, she wonders if The Twilight Man can excavate
the floor of Georgia and compass his way to her body.

Will he atlas until he finds her? Yelps from their babies
leak out from in between the white noise sizzles

of her radio gut. She clings to the crying ricochet bubbling
sick against her organs. This is her boxing ring—

the night's eye, the bloody contest of motherhood & safety. She swings
for her pillow, nightmare wrangling, ripening from the inside out.

The Twilight Man's voice trickles over her belly's wavelength again.
This time, it's closer to her skin: ANN, I KNEW IT. THAT IS YOU.

TUPELO GRANNY WAITRESSES

Atlanta, Georgia, 1949

She waitresses in the same way she loves—like a knife.
She's sharp, but half of the time Tupelo Granny serves
up a blunt end between the *honeys* and *darlins* she spits for tips.

Sometimes, her mind is an issue. The boss
scolds Tupelo Granny when she curses
closing-time customers & gross lunchtime men

gabbing thick & grubbing toward her ass.
But, if anyone in the steel polished pink diner
knew Tupelo Granny's past, they'd pray forgiveness.

In the morning downtime, she leans on the counter,
buffing a rag in circles, all messy with guilt. She thinks
in poems that flower big like *kudzu* and *magnolia*. Thinks

of her blood welded in Mississippi with The Twilight Man.
Tupelo Granny dreams of fleeing back in time, snatching
her babies in the night and returning to her new life in Georgia.

I'd raise 'em right, she tells herself, even though she knows
they've likely already built venomous pools in their guts
for her. She knows The Twilight Man has the babies brainwashed,

that they're no longer *her* clay to cast, but she fantasies
in a matrix of small hopes: the unsent letters under her mattress,
the two-year-old photos wedged in her purse, a future death of

The Twilight Man & her intrepid return to Tupelo.
She dreams of his stillness, his violent limbs sick & sewn
into the earth—all the anger evaporated from his jaw.

She sees bloody stitches crossing his body in zigzags, his fists
hogtied behind his back, the most helpless he's ever been.
She sits pretty in this hallucination until the bell strikes reality,

& she stares green into the eyes of pie-hungry diners. She flips
a switch, rewires her veins & cuts full blade:

Whad'yall want?

YOU ARE GIVING ME SOME OTHER LOVE

Atlanta, Georgia, 1949

In the diner, Wishbone Poppy bangs the loudest drum,
his ballooning laugh & yellow mouth hanging high
above the coiling ripples of midday rush chatter.
He spills heavy & skewers his buddies over coffee,
flagging down Tupelo Granny like she's some idling taxicab.
Wishbone Poppy talks at her different though—
in jasmine vines—his words fleshing out to her in ringlets.
In those quick lushing moments, it's as if Tupelo Granny
is teleported back to the planet before The Twilight Man.
All the budding fevers: a forgotten garden growing like stairs.
Wishbone Poppy is her ultraviolet pill, a reserve unseen.
It's there, in those first seconds of movement, that she feels,
really *feels*, digging her fingers into the earth's blue gravel love.

IF I NEVER SEE THE SETTING SUN AGAIN

Atlanta, Georgia, November 1950

Tupelo Granny lets shame kiss her down. She swims in it now, after all the years she spent miming erasure in Georgia. Her hurt is coated in paranoia, but with Wishbone Poppy by her side, The Twilight Man can't paint her body blue anymore.

The two get hitched in mystery—inside a jerry-rigged church, they share the dusk of carnage in their nuptials. Their wedding might not be official in the eyes of God, but this is elopement. This is shelter. This is chainmail love.

Tupelo Granny knows being half a woman isn't pretty, but Wishbone Poppy doesn't care. Even in the death of night, he makes do with faith. She's the kind of turbulent paradox he invites to be his home. Her fire smolders even stronger when the wind blows south. To Wishbone Poppy, she glows electric in the flat cream of humanity.

When she feels it's time to get moving again, Tupelo Granny & Wishbone Poppy spread thin and make way toward the Hudson. On their voyage north, the snow beams clean against Tupelo Granny's chest. She rewilds over & over in the quiet, hypnotizing stillness of the flurries—becoming full again.

AN ONLY MOON

"Had she not lain on that bed with a boy
All those years ago, where would they be, she wondered.
She and the child that wouldn't have been but was now
No more. She would know nothing
Of mothering. She would know nothing
Of death. She would know nothing
Of love. The three things she'd been given
To remember. Wake me up, please, she said,
When this life is over. Look at her—It's as if
The windows of night have been sewn to her eyes."

—Mary Jo Bang, "Ode to History"

SHADES OF PINK

Perth Amboy, New Jersey, 1961

Her third pregnancy felt like cheating. After all, there were babies in Mississippi plotting her return. But after Wishbone Poppy shipped back from Korea & worked for a couple years, Tupelo Granny began to feel the bliss of safety & let her skin pink under his touch. She blushed in fandango, felt the walls bloom vermillion. Over the molten summer months, her belly swelled toward the moon, & the creature inside her kicked at night, as if she wasn't the right version of *home*. As if she wasn't even part of the right galaxy.

In November, Tupelo Granny rained it all out. In the delivery room, she dressed herself in blood, & the voices inside of her spelled THIS IS PASTEL, THIS IS CAMEO, THIS IS CRIMSON in haunting unison. She pushed the creature out into the world, praying in waves against some genetic curse. When the nurse handed over the sobbing baby boy, Tupelo Granny looked at him like salvation. Like the answer to the shadowy cave she carved out from her chest.

She named him Eddie. He was her second chance—the place where she would undo the traces of desertion she engraved on her other babies, the same traces her momma left her with at 14. She swaddled Eddie like a gemstone in the scratchy cotton of a newly knitted rose afghan & rocked him, cooing sweet vows. Just as she had the first two times around. But this time, Tupelo Granny was gonna make it right. She had to.

METHOD ACTING

Manasquan, New Jersey, 1965

When the phone flees the cradle, Tupelo Granny flees her truth. She slips into character before picking up—flutters through a timeworn vocal warm-up: lip buzz, siren, solfège.

Her cloying *Hellllllo?* blushes through the static, her past life on the other line. It beckons to her, asks her how she is, where she is, what she's been up to.

Tupelo Granny smells the lucidity. The painful façade of concern. She starts to run through her lines like the diva she really is:

We went on vacation finally, a camping trip, which was really great for us. We took a train, and Eddie loved it. And we're moving next month to another house, somewhere bigger, somewhere better.

The words she spits are formless and vague by design. She's good, the family is good, it's all just *good*. Tupelo Granny knows to leave out the specifics. To stretch her dream world into a hazy picture of American perfection.

She goes on for hours, playing the role she knows her past wants for her. Even though the family had never gone camping, had never taken a train, she dives heart first into the details.

Oh, and it was wonderful, all those pine trees, and the beautiful red birds waking me up each morning. We roasted dinner over a fire—the real deal.

Tupelo Granny never tells her past why she's moving for the fifth time in two years. It isn't because she's chasing a bigger house, or a better neighborhood, or the green dream of security.

She wakes in hiding. On the run from a wild yesterday which lurks in the blood of the babies she let Mississippi take. She carries this dishonor in her chest like a purple heart, as if she wounded the earth by saving herself.

Eddie listens to his mother speak in fables & stays quiet. He is witness to her spiraling eclipse—spy to her incredible performance. The kind of performance to which only a broken starlet could commit.

HOMECOMING

Tupelo, Mississippi, 1965

The first time Eddie met Lula
she was bombed & sloppy,
lying listless on a bare mattress
in a lonely Tupelo tenement.

He was five & it was the first time
he felt the small tree of kin glow
in his chest. It was a real-time
shimmer, not like the slow burn

of tumors or Tupelo Granny's
Lucky Strikes. It was fast & warm
like the belly of his daddy's Galaxie
purring wild. Eddie stared

at Lula, the handful of empty bottles
scattered around her like décor, her head
kicked back in laughter & two thick legs
wide open, catching all the summer air.

The world crawled dense in those seconds.
When the slow motion came to a halt,
Eddie's parents whisked him away like morality
& told him to forget it all. But he couldn't

slash that strange glitter from his heart.
The three rode away into the blue & misgiving
Mississippi night, Eddie piecing the puzzle together,
clinging to the new love he named *family*,

while Tupelo Granny let it all hang out:

*Don't get your hopes up, baby. She's nothing to us
right now. She doesn't even know who you are.*

MAKE DO

Wilmer, Alabama, 1966

In the inky blue dusk, Lula sends five-year-old Eddie to collect eggs from the backyard coop. He runs wild across the mule-plowed field toward the faint echo of chicken yelps, his feet kicking back humid storms of soil into the half night. Once inside the coop, Eddie spots the eggs and starts gathering them in his shirt basket by twos. And then the red starts flushing—then, the pouring hoot—the wilted pecking order.

Out from a dark corner, a dippy rooster careens toward him and declares some twisted war. When Lula catches Eddie's hollers from across the farm, she flashes with urgency for the coop. She arrives and Eddie immediately dishes: *It attacked me, Granny!*

Lula grabs the rooster by his sandy feather scruff. With her hardened hands, she wrings the bird's neck in one swift clap. Eddie gapes at his granny and the spilling muscle of her indifference. This is her intuitive armor, her reliable security. The honey of her family. Lula snuffs and spits, collects the rooster's corpse, and beckons toward Eddie: *c'mon, baby, let's have supper. Forget those eggs. This'll make do.*

HALF STITCH

Wilmer, Alabama, 1967

When Eddie got done burning trash out back of the family home, Uncle Huck declared he'd be taking them for a spin in Wishbone Poppy's new car. Huck was a tanked-up drunk half-cut from the same cloth as Tupelo Granny. He came from Lula's second marriage, steeped in the dark underbelly of Alabama for two decades too long.

In his late afternoon stupor, Huck plopped Eddie in the Galaxie's front seat, slapped a seat belt on him & started to fly. They buzzed high on the freeway, uncle whooping & spitting like an over-oiled machine. Eddie's belly surged red & he felt the blot of this landscape creeping up 95 miles fast. He closed his eyes & sunk into that flush. It was Huck's turn to play God.

Then came the tree. And the tailspin. And the flip onto Rt. 98. When Eddie opened his eyes, he was yelping shoeless, standing on the ceiling of the car. Huck's hand reached in the upside-down window & ripped Eddie free. The four-lane was stopped dead, folks running to help. In a snap, Huck threw Eddie's limp body over his shoulder like a sack and walked over to another man's car. Huck blew fat & nasty & ordered the man to bring him to his momma's house. Wordlessly, the man shrunk & complied, his eyes stonefed as onlookers called Huck back to the scene. Eddie felt the world shrink harsh in that moment. He sat silent in the back seat and let the wind drown out his uncle's three-sheet tongue.

Back at home, Huck laid down & Eddie hit shock, spiking a fever in the hundred-degree night. But the law was looking for Huck, so Lula said NO HOSPITAL. Eddie sat there, middle of July, wrapped in a wool blanket, shivering 'til night grew tall. Wishbone Poppy cursed under his breath & promised Eddie they'd never go back to Bama, not even to stop for a piss.

And when the State Trooper came knocking at midnight, Lula didn't say a word. She simply pointed toward the bedroom where Huck lie asleep. The cop hit him awake with a nightstick, dragged him out to the car by his hair, and disappeared into the blotchy Wilmer sky. While Tupelo Granny packed their bags, Eddie watched the naked scene unfurl with shrunken pupils, hoping that Huck got what was coming to him, unaware of the lawless power tracing the cicada night. Of the haunting, inherited tidal crashing before him.

IN ORBIT

Manasquan, New Jersey, 1970

On Saturdays, 9-year-old Eddie woke early to haunt the train line
from Manasquan to Bay Head. He would skulk the secluded depot,
a daybreak phantom probing the liminal for some other friendship.
Eddie would ride solo to the junction yard, snapping blurry photos.
He loved to watch the railcar convoys, speeding in thick strings
of steel toward different portals of life—different harbors of home.
Inside the passenger cars, Eddie felt almost impermanent, his body
hidden in streams of movement, reaching for the life ephemeral.
The railroad workers looked after him, finding light in his endless
questions. They let Eddie go as far as he wanted, cruising electric
on the locomotive, his chest flashing deep with wonder & belonging
until dusk wrenched the sky red with time & he biked home.

*

Tupelo Granny loved to shop. Every Sunday for years, she'd drag
Eddie to Alexander's department store. She'd bask in the material—
mulberry silk, cashmere, fox fur & mink. Even though Tupelo Granny
had nowhere to go, she wanted it *all*. She spent hours in the dressing
room, glittering before the mirror, each outfit a new possibility,
a former or future life. After a few hours, little Eddie would pitch fits
over boredom & aching feet, but Tupelo Granny couldn't care less.
She stood before her reflection, lazing in the imaginary, praying ritual
for a shift in dimension. This was her escape, her hiding place. While
the Twilight Man shifted in her belly, she could still be luminary there,
fitting herself for stardom. Eddie would bellow low for her retreat, but
Tupelo Granny only remained stationary, flitting light between the waves.

*

When the family moved downstate to Brick, Tupelo Granny
told Eddie, *go find a friend*, so he saddled his bike & rode all over,
twined to the rough fantasy of a brand-new sidekick. Eddie
hunted beachside, combing the sand for the wind of another soul.
He trolled the playground, but instead of a friend, he found a village
of lost ghosts. They whispered in allure, a field of strange hosts,
bouncing on the seesaw, riding the spring-borne horses. He laid
down next to one on the carousel, and they spun upside down
like ragdolls for hours. His head swelled messy with inertia & blood.
This became a ritual for him. A prayer against isolation. A plea
to the deity which named him an only moon. And he absorbed
solitude as power, with time & gravity, deep in the mud.

AN ONLY MOON

From Eddie, for Meryl, & Barry

I met my sister in 1971. I was 10 years old.

Even though I always asked a whole lot of questions, my mother treated yesterday like contraband, tucking the memories of Kiln babies under her flattened mattress, spoon-feeding me half-truths until my curiosity ran dry. It took her a decade to find the grit of new genesis. And until then, I hungered for brothers & sisters, for a strand of history to forfeit the double blind.

The day Meryl finally came to visit, my mother ran around the house with a feather duster, hitting the roof all flushed & blabbing in nervous streams. I knew this was a different kind of hell storm. From the first word Meryl muttered, I could tell she was my blood. It pounded inside my chest like telepathy. She stood towering in the sunken living room, her cheekbones riding high like my momma's. Her toothy smile the same glossy gold.

We rode the train into the city together & climbed to the top of the Empire State Building—somewhere my parents would never take me. And there, on the observation deck, 102 stories in the sky, time became a temperamental façade. It spun me into an alternate universe rife with possibility. My map was a flashing light that had been drawn for me far before I was born. Safe from proxy, I breathed blue.

We looked down on the shrunken enormity of 34th St., the extent of our magnitude relative & now related—two giant comrades running parallel on a genetic current. And I felt close to Meryl, like she had always been with me. Like she was *something* to me.

I wish I could still find her.

BOOGIE DOWN, ST. ROSE

Belmar, New Jersey, 1975

Disco Lady, Misty Blue, Squeezebox, the Lowdown, a Livin' Thing—it *all* reigned like magic for Eddie on the night of the school dance. Giddy at the hope of dancing with somebody, he showered nice & dressed tenfold, a bone in his shoes & clothes crisp like winter melody. He decked himself in a sharp number: hair combed, straight slacks, baby blue button down & pumas, green 'n' grey. It was the Boogie Down at St. Rose & he was poised for the sunshine to groove all night long.

In the school gymnasium, the raggedy band played like ready money, the rivets of their chords singing fortune to the shallow night sky above. While his friends beamed in shimmies toward the music, he looked toward the bleachers & studied the many couples sharing quiet talk in the shadows. His chest panged with lightning to have a hand in something like that.

But, like most dances, the Boogie Down was just an exercise in buddy-love, the kind where Eddie's feet flocked in murmurations of their very own. So, this was his getaway. That night, he danced dream funk with the stars & rode a sky-high midnight rollercoaster of purple back home. And, more often than not, this song was all he needed—his guide, *his* tune.

TUPELO GRANNY, PAPER DOLL HOT MESS

Manasquan, New Jersey, 1976

With the smoldering butt of a bogie flapping between her lips, she fastens
a tattered platinum wig atop her wrinkled forehead and vainly applies a 13th coat

of her trademark burnt-apricot rouge. She smacks her mouth and slurs to herself:
Purrrrfect, posing before the vanity mirror like a tanked Jayne Mansfield

at a sloppy pin-up shoot. She climbs in the Thunderbird & floors it through sleepy Manasquan,
cackling like a drunken lead-foot witch flying amidst the tranquil coast-town darkness.

Even in her stupor, she knows she's late to pick up 14-year-old Eddie & his first date
from a party down in Brick. On Ridge Road, her tires screech to a halt, and she stumbles

out of the driver's side door onto the lush, suburban front lawn. She yelps, *Y'all,
I'm here to pick up my baby Eddie, where's he at?* into the night's creaking jar fly abyss. She sighs.

As she makes her way toward the front door, Eddie and his date emerge from the house,
relieved to finally see her foolish grin. But as she looks up to greet him, Tupelo Granny trips

on a loose stone and collapses—launching her faux, shiny locks across the manicured grass.
She lies there, bald and hooting for a few moments until she grows quiet. Her smile gently fades,

and she passes out. This is the most loveable part of her. Without hesitation, Eddie collects his mother and places her slumbering body in the backseat. Distant, he drives both of the women home

and parks the car neatly in the family garage. In the solemn night, he tucks his body into the folds of his mother's, and together they sleep off the binge in the backseat, warm but still shivering.

WHO NEEDS TO PRAY?

Manasquan, New Jersey, 1981

In the stain of July, 20-year-old Eddie takes a thrill ride
on his fat yellow cruiser—round the cemetery, float bar,

boardwalk, downtown. His little Walkman rains & riffs
with *Wild Gift* 'til his legs can't anymore. Once home

he steals away into the alley for a smoke & catches eye
of Tupelo Granny steaming through the kitchen window.

Nobody could fold cloth napkins with anger as she could.
Eddie puts his ear to the siding & hears his daddy

painting the walls red with words about the church:
He's dead, and now God'll have us back. We can finally marry.

Eddie, like any good Catholic boy, feels his father's words
scatter his belly. What were his parents, if not married?

He knew they always followed communionless in the pews,
& he didn't think anything of it, of what came before him.

Tupelo Granny's face twists as she speaks with thunder:
God didn't want me when I wanted him, running all that blue.

She keeps on folding, her hands pulling the cloth taut
with precision. Images of wedding the Twilight Man

flare through Tupelo Granny's brain. St. James Church,
once her home, birthed the union which broke her back.

Back then, her prayers leaked thick like last-ditch colors,
but no divine son could have saved her from that muddy place.

She always thought the image of that man's lifeless body
would bring a new dawn, but her chest echoed hollow & blue

with loss. She stands there, and Eddie watches her,
creasing over. She's inside of herself now—her round face ablaze

with resolve in the spill of the late day's terracotta afterglow:
I'll marry you again. But tell me, who the hell needs to pray?

IVY MATH

"This is where you leave me.
Filling of old salt and ponderous,

what's left of your voice in the air.
Blue honeycreeper trashed out

to a ragged wind, whole months
spent crawling up this white beach

raked like a thumb, shucking, swallowing
the sea's benediction, pearled oxides.

Out here I am the body invented naked,
woman emerging from cold seas, herself

the raw eel-froth met beneath her tangles,
who must believe with all her puckering

holes. What wounds the Poinciana slits
forth, what must turn red eventually."

—*Safiya Sinclair, "Confessor"*

I WAS BORN

late in blue night from roots buried like bodies beneath the high piles
of rusted steel shipping crates stacked on the Jersey Turnpike sideline;

beneath the ricochet of the drowned river valley and its foul water lullaby,
a glimmering baby snake swimming softly in a supple, pearlescent eggshell;

early on salt-stained streets, melting dirty ice mounds into frozen cubbies
where Hudson children lay in solace, like a quiet, drowsy slumberherd;

among the thorny brush of the well park framed with whitewater falls
and dying candyland trees waiting to be carved into small faith homes;

hiding from the Mississippi Kiln inside a corroded chaos teapot, gripping
a bouquet of pink and white bleeding hearts praying for hushed hope time;

falling like hot rain from a goddess body, ripe in strawberry twilight,
hurting for the water bowl's spilling over, for the swelling lilac tufts;

in the green sky of Louisiana flood storms, an unending overflow
cracking the sky, sprouting the crawls of jasmine bulbs in the summer dusk;

swaddled in wiry, heart-shaped honeyvine, throbbing and spread
like the red moon planted high above a mangrove swamp bed;

in wading sickness. I keep on digging in the desperate gulf moonlight
for a dry seed plotted in the rocky soil—my body, the dirt, in pieces.

SMALL ANGRY MAMA

Bayonne, New Jersey, 1998

carelessly turns up the volume dial in her drifting '94 Aerostar
to muffle the summer tantrums howling from the backseat.

Even with the windows down, the restless Hudson dog days cling to her
like a hot skin, and she floors the van down Avenue C. wildly

singing along to *Frampton Comes Alive!* over wind-butchered wails.
She knows you can't find much cold or free inside Bayonne's July—

instead, she savors the taste of a fast ride. Her confused four-year-old cries:
Mommy, where are we going? and Small Angry Mama hisses back: *Crazy!*

as she speeds into the Quik-Chek parking lot to buy a Coke slushie and finally light up.
But, by the filter hit, it's almost shift time at the Big Apple & she leaves for home.

She drives, hanging high over the port city like the Bay's nightfall smog,
fluttering in thick waves of afterglow until the sunshine runs dry.

THE GOODNESS

is what my granny liked to call the top layer of her cobbler—
that cloying, salted brown sugar crumble that sang lyrical
against the roof of my mouth. Even though I thought that word,
goodness, was only reserved for foods with actual nutritional value,

I kept my mouth shut & full of the divinity she taught me.
Soon, I realized that goodness was in *everything* I loved: butter cookies,
baked mac 'n' cheese, sweet peas, even cornbread dressing.
And I started to wonder why nobody else cooked with goodness—

after all, it was the sole ingredient that always made my entire family
croon a loud choir of *mmmm*'s at dinner time. My dad used it sparingly,
only when recreating one of granny's recipes, scribbled on the backside
of an index card, like her drop biscuits or cobbler. But I could always taste

the difference. Now, I know that it's because goodness is not just
an item on a recipe list. It's not like vanilla extract, eggs, butter.
It's not like candied fruit. It's the dirty combination of it all,
the whole network of goods & a metamorphosis of their meaning.

It's a special type of nourishment, one with an evolution,
one which speaks in familiar whispers to the inner parts of you,
one where the honey air, humanity of family, flour and Crisco
are all mixed in & rebirthed with a new name. A better name.

WHEN I WAS FOUR (TO BE SEEN & NOT HEARD)

Bayonne, New Jersey, 1998

When I was knee-bruised and exploding like yellow from my mouth. When my body was all punches and stiff kisses. When my belly started to feel like a hill to climb. When I wasn't ready for the rain to come. I was a soldier living for combat and He taught me the alphabet of silence. At first, I thought it was a game, hide-and-seek—I spit my words out backward, my throat spellbound & tangled. I stopped asking questions. Instead, my fingers grew toward a creation of answers: the sky wasn't blue, the walls all had headaches, there weren't any trees. Colors existed only on paper, only to be whispered between me & whatever figure of God I was taught to love. That world was like underwater, like a chamber of safety, free of gravity and noise. I swam alone. I washed my face in that type of wilt—all my new scars were absorbed into that chamber. The game became an exercise in consumption. I ate my words. But I wish I could tell Him now: *If you cut out my tongue, I will write you a letter.* I wish I could tell Him: an animal's thoughts don't spill like logic; the magic of coral can't be undone. I am not seasonal; I cannot drift out to sea like this.

OUR MUSIC

Bayonne, New Jersey, 2000

I'm the boss. I make all the rules. Monica loves dresses, and I hate them. Still, Mom makes us wear the same outfit, like twins, even though I'm oldest. We lock arms and spin and spin and spin. Some days we tear into the cabinets and take the pots & pans hostage. Monica bangs them hard and fast, like the leader of our two-man band. I play the cheese grater while she sings green heaven.

I sit Monica on the counter and spread peanut butter all over her body. She is my early canvas. When Mom finds us, she laughs and takes pictures for when we grow up. We smile to the moon for the home videos. I want to grow up and be the bear in the big blue house. Monica wants to sing and scream like Robert Plant on the big stage. We 10-second-tidy and I pour water all over her head.

Monica and I forge worlds in the backyard, where we capture pill bugs and keep them as pets in a makeshift terrarium. I rip up the grass in clumps and stick it inside the cage so the bugs can eat good. Sometimes we pretend to be dogs named Biscuit and Butter, since we don't have one yet. In the winter, I stand atop the porch steps and declare myself King of December Brats. I roll Monica in the falling powder and expect her to become a snowball.

At night, we create shadow puppets and make them kiss. We give them romances. When it's time for bed, I throw the flashlight across the room so Monica can use it as a night light. I break the lamp in the process. We lie to Dad and say it just exploded, and for some reason he believes us. Monica asks me how I breathe so quietly when I sleep, and after a while of talking, she shushes me to bed. *Don't break my silence*, she whispers, *I'll see you in dream world. We can talk there.*

LUCKY

Small Angry Mama skirts
down Broadway toward Brick City
in her Aerostar, her unamused
six-year-old daughter in tow.

She sings *Rosalita*
until her face goes ruddy
and flicks a glowing joint butt
out the window into the dulled,
tired slush lining the city streets.

She passes Bayonne's gems
like a callous raven at night,
airborne and soaring. They glimmer
in the streetlight fog, one by one:

Abramson's Jewelers, the creaky
old laundromat, Hudacko's pharmacy,
the brand new, supersized Blockbuster.
Her daughter, lulled in the backseat, stares

at the buildings humming by,
spots McDonald's, and yelps
like a hungry puppy: *Mommy! I want fries!*
Small Angry Mama doesn't skip a beat:
No fries, tonight, baby. I have to pay the electric bill,
and pulls into a gas station.

She eyes the storefront's flashing neon
Mega Millions sign. It speaks to her.
She prays in numbers, slips
out of the van and disappears.

Minutes later, she runs out of the minimart,
waving a scratch-off ticket, dancing
in the winter drizzle. She screams, *I won baby!
Four-hundred-and-change!* while skipping
through the dingy parking lot.

In a beeline she floors it
toward the McDonald's drive-thru,
the Bayonne snow-sludge hissing

behind her. She orders two large fries,
hands one to her daughter, and whispers:
I've always been lucky, baby.

I CAN STILL HEAR THE NIGHTS WE DREAM

    for Monica

& my little sister singing in my brainwaves—
the corals inside her skull blooming
the fragile & unnamed mental science
dogging me in the deep night.

The corals inside her skull blooming,
she swims me to the very bottom
dogging me in the deep night.
Holding my mind like a guide, her eyes rainless,

she swims me to the very bottom.
Her songs pierce sonar in that blue,
holding my mind like a guide,
and I test her with my loud, with my fear.

Her songs pierce sonar in that blue, too,
and nothing hurts more than this trust.
Holding my mind like a guide, her eyes rainless,
our hearts flashing together in code.

And nothing hurts more than this trust.
The fragile & unnamed mental science,
our hearts flashing together in code.
My little sister singing in my brainwaves.

TUPELO GRANNY SLEEPS, WISHBONE POPPY WAKES

Bay St. Louis, Mississippi, 2001

Once, there was a woman who slept draped in flames of wine. The flames snaked in bruises around her slumbering body like diamondbacks, hissing coals toward the ear of God. They told him of pigs rolling in the thick mud of her belly, all the bulletproof-ness she preached. And the woman lay rock-still in this bed, a cigarette smoldering in her unconscious hand, the whole scene praying to the sky for divine intervention.

But wasn't it God who gave her awful habits like eating the overcast of stars at night, or smoking Virginia Slims in bed? And wasn't it God who looked down on the image of this sleeping woman & whispered *shh now, let's leave her be?*

He sung to the fire in coaxing bellows & the fire, like any good, charmed serpent, did just as it was told.

The woman, nearing suffocation, stood in an empty field, shooting a rifle at the sky in her dreams. She shot & shot & shot, screaming devotions at the clouds, like *this one's for the time Huck almost killed me, and this one's for you, Ma,* until the ammo ran dry.

The woman fell to her knees in this dusty, barren pasture, and took stock of the graveyard of lead before her. She felt pleasure knowing she learned to mimic the language of violence before it ever got to swallow her. And through this dream, she slept, enveloped in the red glow of rising smoke, ignorant of her own near death.

But what God forgot was the man sleeping down the hall in his separate bedroom, who woke like a paragon in the night's peak to use the bathroom. He spotted the smoke furling in rattles from under the woman's door & broke through the lock she had installed.

The man quickly opened a window to vent the vapors, and the room instantly burst into a hellfire, an abyss. With the flames taunting his flesh & the woman—the anchor which held him—he scooped up her still-sleeping body, the miniature poodle beside her & the keys to his station wagon.

With the woman & puppy in the backseat, the man floored the gas and reversed the car out of the garage, watching the fire engulf the house completely. He gawked at the plague of it all & let the earth starve him.

The man looked upon the woman, needled with fear like a bat lost in music, flying blind toward zero. The woman lay unphased through it all, sleeping heavy in the wagon's backseat.

And once she was safe, wasn't it God who laughed in flocks like a banshee, reading the song of her fate? Wasn't it He who kept her dragging on the slims until her brain bought a farm for itself? Wasn't it He who gave pet names to her curse, cooing in the night?

That's when the man learned expiration; when the woman finally woke & heard God bawl in tongues of pain.

In a raven song, she began to croon a metamorphosis—a new shadow. And as mold grew deep around the man's pruning heart, she just kept on chanting louder toward the flickering, soundless wind: *Go, baby, go.*

I'M IN FLORIDA WITH YOU

Panama City Beach, 2002, after James Fenton

I was 7 when I had my first real vacation. One outside of the sweaty budget apartments in Jersey's Seaside Park where my family went to drink every summer. Granny & Grandpa rented us a house in Panama City Beach for a week, and I was knee-deep in the fantasy of Florida. All my friends always came back from Florida with puka shell necklaces & sunburns that made their sunken faces bloom with life mid-winter. We went in July, and I imagined myself dog day royalty.

My parents drove us the 25 hours down in our janky maroon GMC Suburban. We rode straight through, stopping only to use the bathroom & order at McDonald's. I listened to Ricky Martin's *Sound Loaded* over & over on my Walkman with Monica's stinky feet propped up on the headrest of my seat, catching wind on the highway.

When we got there, the sun rayed through the clouds like homecoming. It splashed waves of ginger & broke clean in a surge of yellow. The gulf was clear & green & the wet, packed sand squeaked under my feet. I didn't notice the trashy main drag littered with Alvin's Islands & other gift shops, or the scum growing thick all over the roadside waterpark. I didn't know better, or that I should care.

It was *Florida*, and I was gonna lap it all up.

On that trip, Granny's love was impeccable. She read to me, took me shopping, whispered secrets like *your daddy is never too old to be scolded by me* in my ear at bedtime. Granny's laugh was a raspy caw that traced through my chest & her puckered, fed-up lips spoke more volumes than an almanac.

And I spent the entire week parroting her, wanting to *be* her, smitten with having *her* as my Granny. I spread her signature lipstick all over my face, trying to mimic her cross-vexed grace. After the vacation was over, we went our separate ways & I, donned in plastic puka shells, stood on the street & waved buh-bye, blowing kisses at my grandparents' station wagon.

Granny didn't look back. She didn't wave back. It was like she didn't even see me, jumping up & down in my glittery flip-flops, screaming for her goodbye in the heavy after-storm air. She just kept her face skewed forward, eyes anchored firm on the road ahead of her, like she was trying to make sense of some mirage I couldn't see. Grandpa hit the gas, and her gaze was locked in as if she knew what was coming. As if she was trying to silently disassemble the watery shadow cast before her.

BELATED ELEGY: MOTH, FLAME

When Wishbone Poppy got his orders for Korea in 1951,
he & Tupelo Granny shipped out to Seattle. On the way

to Seattle, they twanged Cherry from Lula's grasp
down in Wilmer. She was 11 years old, learning

to decipher the blues buried across her palm lines,
& Tupelo Granny was scared to be alone.

It was an early April weekend—the gunmetal
horizon brushed bloodless with spring haze,

& the trio moseyed the ranging plains, humming
to tin whistle country, charmed like lucky serpents

in the dawn of a new order. In Chicago, Cherry
was gifted a little Easter chick & she doted on it,

whispering moonstrikes toward a baby bird
in the damned marrow dialect of her kind.

She kept the chick alive 'til they hit Wyoming,
where it faintly chirped to a sodden stillness

& faded on in her tiny hands. Wishbone Poppy
shouldered the car on highway 90 & Tupelo Granny

handed Cherry her best scarf to wrap the barren
fledgling body. In the gut of a raging snowstorm,

all three knelt roadside & staged a makeshift funeral.
Cherry buried the Easter chick beneath the frost

while Wishbone Poppy sang the liturgy, praying
homeward in the icy tide, and there, in that smudge

of stopgap devotion, they all broke from chrysalis.
Tracing a muddy sanctuary within the overcast,

they joined hands & called out in eulogy—
the sheen of an impermanence now consumed.

SIX WAYS TO PLAY POSSUM

Shelton, Connecticut, 2004

1. I splay my heavy limbs motionless across a bare, twin mattress twice my age. My mind is in half as the rural moonlight bulb seeps through my cracked blinds like a warped-glass ornament.

2. Hoping my body will sink back to sleep, I listen to my parents speak softly in the living room, their tangled whispers rebounding off peeling lilac walls. Their leaden feet dance choreographies of burden in the space between the floor and the handsewn curtain hung in place of my door.

3. My dad sits on the torn emerald leather couch and pulls on his loyal Redbird boots. He is dressed—again, maybe for the hundredth time—for his first day of work as a journeyman electrician. My mom floats through the room, a spirit body in a thin, pale pink nightgown and hands my father a gunmetal thermos.

4. I hear his six-foot-six body slump into the crushed loveseat's give. My mom wraps her short arms around him, forming an incomplete hug. She's brief with her encouragement.

5. I'm silent in back of the house. With my eyes closed, I see my father at work: a lightbulb scientist splicing heart wires, reconnecting fault lines. In the East Village nightshade, his caving whimpers are engulfed by the howls of coyotes and snow winds bashing against one another.

6. I wait for the front door to latch. He has never been so far away, but these are the small hours. He is a giant, a dull blade—a magnolia wedged in the glacier earth. A boom swallow riding a ceaseless train to nowhere.

H-A-Y-T

Big brother taunts me in steamrolls. Mike cackles at my big belly & makes me remember I'm bad at Zelda. He blames me when Mom asks him who broke the rocking chair, so I write MIKE WAS HERE in sharpie on my bedroom walls. He drops ice blocks on my head when it snows.

Mike makes me pay him a dollar every time I ask him to teach me Pokémon. He hit the baseball that knocked out my two front teeth. I cry not because it hurts, but because I'm scared they'll never grow back. I try to trick Mike into burning his hand on the stove, but I forgot he's the one who taught me that trick.

When I log onto the computer to make Mike a greeting card that says I HATE YOU MIKE, Mom won't tell me how to spell hate. So, I click the floral Easter card design, delete the text & improvise: I HAYT YOU MIKE & slip it under his door. When he finally sees it in the morning, he tells me he doesn't hate me and gives me a hug.

Sometimes, Mike plays Barbies with me and he lets me put dresses on G.I. Joe. He still wears camo pants under everything but looks prettiest in yellow. It's weird because I hate dressing Barbie, but I love dressing Joe. And the best part is that Mike doesn't mind.

WHITE NOISE

Got any 2's?

> I'm lying on the living room carpet during a thundersnow as the bitter winds fight like bobcats in the Valley night. It's a blackout & we're playing go-fish.
>
> With the help of a battery-powered Milwaukee radio, my family is listening to the blaring stylings of Jethro Tull's *Aqualung* (for the third time today).
>
> As the radio begins to crackle, my father gets up, tells me, *Go fish*, and I draw a queen from the deck, waiting for his queue.
>
> My father is preoccupied, fiddling with his stereo and   pointing the antenna in every direction, hoping to salvage the signal, but there is only white noise.
>
> Frustrated, he surrenders and turns the volume dial, shutting out sound. I put my hand of cards on the floor and study the industrial radio.

What's Milwaukee?

> With the flashing frost plague of blue storm light cast against his back, he explains, *Milwaukee is a city in Wisconsin, famous for almost nothing.*
>
> The jade sky cracks and bellows like an unfolding hunger boom and my father's voice, a familiar whisper, leaks into the dark, sullen room: *famous for nothing, except a cannibal.*
>
> Hail and snow crash to the ground in tall clusters, their girth trapping us inside like penned babies, and I ask him: *What's a cannibal?*
>
> He tries to explain: *it's eating your own kind, a sort of desperation*—but mid-sentence, he looks over at my tiny, disapproving mother and stops. He turns to me and asks, *Got any kings?*

WISHBONE POPPY

lived in our basement for years after Tupelo Granny passed—
after her second stroke, after she burned down their forever-home
perched deep in the Kiln by smoking Virginia Slims in bed

and falling asleep. Wishbone Poppy was rescued by my father from the gummy squalor hotel,
their crude makeshift home, tar-stained like a beaten path ashtray.
As his father wept in the spoil, my father cleaned and brought him north

to the creaking Valley hills. He treated us grandbabies to Burger King on weekends,
made a trailer-home girlfriend, slept on a mattress with a sunken middle,
and bought plastic wine glasses. He would pass out with a drink

in hand, and we would find him the next day, snoring in crimson bleach,
the unbroken glass on the floor. At night, he would race through White Hills
on a cloud, drunk and scatting to jazz songs in his shoddy Chrysler Sebring.

One night in January, he wrecked into a fire hydrant and called my father in the small hours to help him tow out. In his basement home, he would boil whole chickens, rip out their bones, and feed the dark, mucky meat to his Dachshund-Poodle, Dolly.

The stench of poultry would waft up through our home's thick summer air, making the night dense and sour. In secret, he'd hand the greasy clavicles to us grandbabies, and whisper faintly: *Make me a wish, y'all. Make me a growing tree— a seed plotted far from here.*

VALLEY BLUE

"Last night we killed a possum,
out of mercy, in the middle of the road.

It was dying, its face was bloody,
the back legs were shattered. The mistake

I made was getting out of the car
(you told me not to), but I wanted to be

Sure, needed to know for sure, that it could
not be saved."

—*Ada Limon, "In The Country of Resurrection"*

SHE CHANTS AT MY SLEEPING BODY

Questions from Tupelo Granny stain my dreams like snowstroke typography—the broadheaded letters peer at my brain like scattered stars. She beckons for more voice, wants to comb my thoughts. Wants to radio into this reality. She wants in crossing lines and waves, not capital. She wants a heart. One that doesn't beat like mine. Tupelo Granny shoots symbols into the dark of my slumber, and some nights, when she comes to me, it's all math: plus this & minus that patterning my flushing mindflakes. We solve for variables together. She's my walking stick. But, other nights, I wait and wait in the fold of the Valley, like a moth shaking at the moon for more questions. She guides me into the blue space, but unlike her ghost, the questions won't return.

STEWING

I'm 9 years old and Wishbone Poppy just moved into our basement from Mississippi. In summer night, he drinks boxed wine next to his open window and sings in drunk butchered French. Bathes in the faint chirps of tree frogs. I think Tupelo Granny would hate it here, but he tells me he loves the country of it all.

*

Wishbone Poppy's white Chrysler is brand new & rips through the hills like fast colors. He takes me on thrill rides—down Birdseye, 110, the narrow road next to the Stevenson dam—the raceways of the dark side. We tear down the Valleyscape, howling in the gloom.

*

One night, in the shade of winter, we skate wild across the black ice, jazzing along to some unknown cassette. On a hilltop, Wishbone Poppy slams the Chrysler's tires to a yelp & parks. He lowers the music and steps out into the cold, hushing me.

I peek out over the windshield to see him in the pit of night, stalking a mutant possum. It drags sick legs behind its body. My grandpa is barehanded & hunting. And the possum is playing blue. But, right when Wishbone Poppy's hand belts down to snatch the possum, it scurries into the nightfog like the better of two animals.

He climbs back into the Chrysler, his brawn fizzling before me. He frowns into my eyes & breathes in January clouds: *You bet I'll make ya that possum stew one of these days.*

*

It's my senior year of high school & I'm jazzing again in Tim's red sedan. It's us against whatever brute birthed the river valley. I'm hissing the malted breath of Wishbone Poppy as we coax the car down 110 at midnight. I close my eyes for a minute, hearing the echo of my laugh buzz like a boom siren. Then, the rush begins.

Tim wrenches the car roadside & screams in bells. I think we're OK, but then the *shits* and *stops* and *hows* start spilling. We scramble out of the car, smoke soaring from the grill, our hair in our hands. It's totaled. Wrecked in the blue.

*

A year before he died, Wishbone Poppy got stewed with his girlfriend Dotty & crashed the Chrysler into a fire hydrant on our neighbor's front lawn. He called the house & spat fire over the line as if it was all the hydrant's fault. I knew it then: Wishbone Poppy was chasing vulture love. His pockets hollow, his flesh fussing in swarms for the final meal.

*

Tim & I sink down to investigate the undercarriage. The axle is broken in two. We shine a flashlight, looking for the reason why, and the unblinking eyes of a maimed possum shine back at us. Its body is wrapped like bloody gum around the wheel.

Under the ivy of night, the beer of my gut is deep and warm. I wonder if the valley, this gash in the planet, is it for me. I swallow my cackle and look to the sky for some direction home. For the comets of Wishbone Poppy. For his smelly possum stew that I never got to try—wafting tall & inert above the alien mess we made.

LILIES OF THE VALLEY

Shelton, Connecticut, 2009

                                          It was Valentine's day.

The moment keeps tripping over itself:
Wishbone Poppy whispering a prayer
in the secret language of flowers—

                                the clutch of his heart, driving forward,
                                a phone call, darkness flitting on the other line,
                                a jug of cheap red wine unfinished.

Three envelopes stuffed with bills for his grandbabies
lay on the mucky tray table in the basement,
notes of forever lost inside.

                                At the hospital, he saw rain in its original form,
                                spinning & spinning until his chest failed,
                                the scream of machines all around him.

His deaf ears squealed gone with time,
but he had waited too long to speak,
and the snow learned his softness.

                                His hands were made of brass & love
                                like a flock of magic sun-stained starlings
                                drawing a map to the end of the earth.

                                He knew that winter only happens
                                when death strikes a deal with the soil
                                so the lilies can be born again.

ON BECOMING WOMAN

The girl stitches her orphan limbs together like memory,
some tissue more elastic, some brittle & undead.

Her legs are two different animals: one, the muscular stilt
of a Calico steed & two, some slender avian invention.

She is the marriage of wingspan & cat claw, the place
where Caiman scales & Lynx love secretly meet.

Even with her ill-assorted anatomy, she takes pride
in her multiplicity, in the craft & muscle that she sows.

She measures her body as a consummation of time—
each organ a flashback machine reeking of instinct.

Is her mouth the wound of nostalgia? Does she
remember a time before the cross stitch of creature?

It's as if she is a patchwork of her own creation,
her physicality a danger embroidered.

As if some negotiation of being sleeps in her belly—
an acid swilling in deluge like the water of all sin.

BLUE MATH

I inherited my father's algebra—
& like his smile or eyes,

it's part of my arithmetic.
Early on, my body learned to mirror

the blue math which pilots his mind.
So, I don't trust my reality, and most mornings

I am the constant, solving for the variables
y or x in equations trying to calculate *risk & ruin*.

I'm well educated in the language of fear,
and sometimes, I can't seem to codeswitch

out of these tongues, or breathe low
through the cavernous median of worry.

My father and I, we're scared of the *could*
painted in the bottomless heart of the earth.

We nightmare over *possibility* and *infinity*,
the catastrophe of noise, of overload,

of being better. I'm nervous that life isn't plastic,
but rather, that it's just a collection of injured hours

where nothing is linear, & I'm always treading water,
working like hell to avoid the inevitable flood.

I can't even drink tequila, wear vented Nike shorts,
celebrate my birthday, or buy groceries

without the alarm of *destiny* blaring in my chest.
I try to fight sound with tangibility,

but studying the tactile can only help so much.
It's like I embody the *what if*, the ever-stemming

overfunction of a hammerhead circling—
swimming endlessly, snared in a perpetual cycle

of shallows. It's the calibration of suspicion
in my genes: the pinpoint I can't identify.

CANNIBAL FLOWER

Shelton, Connecticut, 2011

Kids gather like jackals in the Valley:
inside the stomachs of low cars,
around lanky pallet fires,
all cloaked in a flood of powdery stillness.

        In this secret orbit of inferno night,
        they blow sugar-bleached smoke
        from their mouths, their heads rattling
        a collection of stains swollen red & empty.

    They laugh wildly & ache
    with cold homesickness
    for places they'll never go,
    clutching palm leaves, plotting

        abandon. I sit beside them,
        my mind a warm loop
        blooming and blooming
        until I am another Her.

She lies still on the sodden sponge
of January ground below my feet,
her stench growing out of me,
she-not-me. We shrink in the laughter.

        Will she live here forever?
        In this small badge of night,
        a tucked blue petal?
        How could she feed
        the decomposing fire of her gut
        inside this dead pine?

        I press my fingers into her eyelids
        until a brave pink hibiscus
        swallows a scarlet ghost litter
        of poppies against her eye's interior.

                When I lift my hand from her face,
                she is still closed—her eyes
                still closed, pulsing with screams
                for some soundless sea.

She watches and waits,
like any good heroine
for the cannibal flower to disappear
into a birth of tiny embers

        rooting their way into darkness.

IN THE VALLEY RAINTIME, I AM

full like the hips of field love,
shifting all down low and wet
in a thick storm of lightning bugs.

gasping toward the honey of solitude—
nightblind, my head a veil, buzzing
in tune with the cleansing cricket song.

a mouth stuffed full of mums,
flowering red & unadulterated
in the empty of august sun.

working like the hills don't exist,
piecing together the map of my belly,
the twisted, dewy country vine inside of me.

towering & overgrown—
my thighs, a dormant mossy boulder
eclipsing the edge of seamless woods.

feeding on rust meals, praying
for the satisfied dark melon of the earth
for the hard swallow, the worsening.

haunting the hidden tunnels of sleep,
spiraling & soft & tethered like a ghost:
this place is the pit of my waking.

the she who births nightmares from her chest,
the she who screams in vapors of green,
the body double trapped inside time.

THE HOLE WHERE MY DOOR ONCE WAS

My bedroom doorframe hangs wide open
as if to say *there no longer exists any barrier to intimacy.*

It's a temporal rift in freedom, an eternal window
to incessant family clamor made possible by your

post-shift temper. We slammed the door again
& again, faces flushing 'til the hinges ripped loose.

I try to makeshift privacy by hanging an old shower curtain,
but electric resonance floods through the fabric.

Now, I can't sleep, between the sound of late night
infomercials, the damn cuckoo clock & the ugly chatter

of unrealities hissing contempt at me. With nowhere
to hide in the afternoons, my temp Valley boyfriend

& I thrush noiseless behind the thin cloth drape,
making clouds of dust flutter cross the high sun.

I tell him, *I can't love you in public* & he reminds me:
seclusion is only a farce. Our fear of the communal

is evidence of an experiment-gone-wrong. And I think
I believe him. Maybe we are both just stuck

on the wrong side of the portal. Nobody should revel
as individual. But I suspect his idea of collectivity

is merely a mode of coercion. Our home is dirty sick
& he fell into the ditch a long time ago. I winnow

my phobias & dump him, wondering if this hole
where my door once was has finally imprinted itself

on me. Some nights, the curtain's tension rod fails me,
& I lie there awake, listening to Bobby Mays' voice

hooting on low volume, staring into the naked, dark
gorge that somehow always exists beyond the valence.

WALMART AND OTHER VALLEY HANGOUTS

As puppets, Tim & I traipse the disheveled megastore aisles,
all spiritless & treasure hunting on a Saturday night—

the backwoods definition of fun. We ride kid bikes
with holographic tassels and bounce

giant, translucent dollar balls against the speckled tile.
In the hardware department, we pick up odd ends

like camo duct tape and thick, unraveled spools
of cooking twine. And, as I slurp my melting Frostie,

our cramped fingers dig deep in the movie candy bin,
searching like fire ants for some sweet, biting relief.

When we tire of turning tchotchkes, we hitch a ride to McDonald's,
get sparkly in the parking lot, and wait for the show to start:

coyote boys in their oil-stained carpenter jeans, trashed
& fighting big against the sky's plum dark backdrop.

They swing & holler, and we sit on the drive-thru curb,
no-good smart kids with hungry eyes sharp for blood.

This dance has been rehearsed weekly for as long as I know—
the rainbow line of modded Volkswagens sputtering exhaust,

spiked sweet teas & the smell of burning. The daughters
of the Valley sun whooping on the sideline in denim miniskirts

until the cattle wakes up. The silent enlistment of our birth,
the medicine of winding hills & the spiraling language of deadheads.

It's like church. Valley folk splay out in worship, pray for a gulf
to save them, even though they've got no reason to hold faith.

And somehow, Tim and I wade through the exaltation nightly
to come out the other side, dusk-faced but still alive.

Now, I watch their choreography from an aerial view in the clouds,
the small, aimless bodies moving in faraway patterns like starlings,

and I hear the weekend battle cries echo against the sprawling edges
of our tiny home, sidestepping one another for the nameless escape.

10 MINUTES OF BLUE

blue (n). (v). bluing

1. Opening the world, the valley where the machine once was: a gaping dimple in time. It is without function—an eternal depth waiting for some greening humanity, some cycle of dusk to overtake.

2. The smattering of crisis seeping dark through clouds: the place where family lives. I am swaddled in the small depression of its hollow bosom. I soak my face in this bowl and scrub all my sorry limbs away.

3. Rhythm of joyride; the piercing air of my sister in Aquarius. Cement of indigo birthing your feet; a theory of cow fields; the edges of solitude.

4. The intestines of a comet, their billowing folds. It is here that my skeleton finds topography—the protruding femur, the boneskin holes where a tongue would fit.

5. Granny's nesting dolls buried within each other, buried deep in the attic, only to be uncovered during times of ripe air.

6. A rush unmistakable in the spirals of my mind. I dive in it for canons, for algae, for women, for Tupelo. I breathe it all into my chest & feel my heart ricochet.

7. A knotted dreamscape of life frozen beneath the Hudson's water, engineering a map of possibility. My primal gaze and the intimacy of earth at my feet.

8. Revolution of hue; a burden of gravity undone. My body floating, the crescents of jasmine overtaking me, a shawl of silent floral geometry.

9. Long desiring a retreat of growth; feeding on nightshades, my belly, erotic and hungry; miracle hour; muddy southern patches where the light bleeds out.

10. Studying the curves of night, the tender anatomy; I sleep alone, caressing these bitter fruits nightly; I ask for the blossom in dreamscape.

I STILL SMELL YOU, DISTANCE ASIDE

for dad

Your hate for aftershave—

    I can still smell

        the staccato notes played

from the out-of-tune upright Wurlitzer

        you hauled up the stairs for me.

    It's like the warm, muggy flux

of your coffee breath   coming for me

    after crashing the Honda into a snowbank.

And the forever stain of epoxy

    used in the attic,   on your model train layout,

where I stationed myself   on the musty carpet

    & watched you work.

    Or the stench of oil

on your fingerprints   after we dropped

    the engine

into the chest of your Dodge one-ton.

    I can smell it—

                    the sweat of your apologies,

                            the long midwinter car rides

                    where I learned the map of your memory.

                                    I can smell the dust of your overalls

                    in the after-school sun,

        the deep reverb of your voice

                            singing to wake me for school,

the small of the night

                            when I would listen sleepless

                                    for you to stop breathing   & start again.

        I'll always remember the perfume of fear

                    you let me inherit, the genetic doubt,

                            the everlasting taste.

        Because of this,

                            I still smell it all.

The gravel we were both born from,

                    your enormous calloused hands

                                    & the way they grasp

        the blank air   for my heart.

        Your past lives   your pride   the hole

in your chest, carved out for me.

              Distance aside.

IN WHICH I FINALLY SAY THANK YOU

Your now-widened feet are the evidence of me once cradled inside your scarred belly. The stains of freckles under your eyes are evidence of light, of the morning shore you share with me. The spider veins that sprawl across your thighs trace the outline of blood that torrents us both. You are borderless and messy and unbottled.

I still wish to bury my face in your Bermudan perfume—the one that reeks of sweat and safety, of ice-cream nights & your not-so-hidden fullness. For years, I have lived for this definition of *beautiful*.

> The people who love you always tell me:
> *you work just like your mom.*

But, what they don't know is that I live deep in the ocean you poured for me. I live in debt to your sore body soaking in Epsom. To your language of sacrifice, to the swells of forgiveness you granted me. To your becoming yourself. To all the mistakes you laughed away, a chalice of rum & coke teetering in your small hands.

> I work like you so I can labor a love like you—
> your food always was my food.
> Your hunger, my hunger.

Mom, your chest beats in flashes of lilacs. It beats in hushes like a whisper from the dusk of the earth. It beats, sketching a pattern of roses, the same forged life raft I always knew to expect from you.

TO MY GRANNY

You probably already know, but I finally went back to the Kiln. I sat in the gas station parking lot and thought of your spider veins, the sun in your blood. I went back to the blue—to the sinking swampland playground. I ate jumbo watermelons and boiled peanuts, watched kids play kick-the-can while hurricanes of red dirt eddied through the August air. I thought of your escape, your return. Your husband before grandpa. The babies you were forced to leave behind. The frantic midnight ride to Georgia. The throbbing pieces of you hidden throughout the earth, lying dormant & raw in the river silt like splintered glass. I imagine what it would be like if we could press a record of your memories and play them back: the running dead, an identity change, all the white lies, your lost birth certificate, the throwing knives. Like the broken chicken necks, they're all mythology & blurred lore for me. But, paralyzed in the thick of Mississippi, I wish to inherit storm that brewed inside of you: the one that ricochets inside of me. They all say I look just like you—the hard eyes, sharp teeth, knitted lips. And I know in my chest that we are two serpentine sisters, birthed from the same flow of some angry ancestral foam. I am a mirror of you, slithering in the forest, lost and trying to find a root. Any root. So, I dig, and I dig, and I look, but my hands keep coming up empty. Is this the barren soil of you? Of me?

LOCUST BRIDE

As a child, I spit a peach pit
onto the bed of my father's Dodge one-ton,
and it immediately turned into a locust.
I peered at the locust through the truck's bulky,
rusted rearview and let it hypnotize me.
I let it love me.

> It seemed like the right thing to do.
> After all, before I created the locust,
> it was just a pit inside my mouth,
> scraping against my teeth
> like it wanted to be free.

Now I'm older, and the locust
and I live in marriage.
In the daytime, I go to work
and sometimes I forget about our vows,
but at bedtime, the locust and I lie
down next to each other.

> While we sleep, the moonbeams
> paint a bouquet of affliction
> and the locust buzzes madly,
> caught in twilight's blued thicket.

Once in a while, the locust traces
its wiry wings through my mind
to draft a slumber blueprint.

> The flutters ache in my head
> like a regret balloon,
> and I tell the locust to give it a rest.
> It never does.

I'M GETTING THERE

    by an image of the torn up   my dad says in a text,   his words escorted

Tub gone, vanity scrubbed out,   bathroom floor.

    genuflecting by that old toilet.   I think of my teenage shins   tile imprinted & sticky,

    searching for its body of water.   My head a starving, spinning glacier

and, still, I clone myself.   I remember thinking, *I'm taller than the mirror*

    wilting miasmas did I birth on that cold tile?   I'm banyan, 15-years-old, counting my past lives.   How many

    an oyster shell of someone-to-be   Back then, I was a marbled carcass

    praying past the cloud which clung to my skin.

    The bathroom was inoperative for the last 10 years.   It's headway—I get it.

Stones in my stomach,   how many drowning machines   did I build in that bath?

Back then, I was just as much   construction as I am now,

    my fingers constantly forging   ugly truth with the fallen-thru baseboards.

Delete it all, the map of my worship.   The fleeting cast of my mutation.

THE DIRT WHICH BIRTHS US

Foxworth, Mississippi, 2021

At the bottom of Red Bluff, I see you. Your body an eggshell, your insides spilling out like yolk across the sunset clay. I see your muddy boots abandoned at the bottom of the canyon, your face covered in pink dirt. I see you tied to a tree like a faded bandana, flapping in the breeze. I see you spinning out in the four-wheeler-made-waterfall, wrapped up in the gnarled mess of deflated tires.

I see you in a gauzy yellow nightgown, wading out into the mouth of the Pearl River. I see you detach your feet and escape the mucky silt. I see you in the way the water forges its own strategy. I see you on the train tracks, hurtling like a coyote in your slippers toward the abandoned trainwreck.

I see you in all that hasn't escaped this giant cavern. I see you scaling the walls of the bluff with your hair wrapped up—self-done nails scratching mad at the sandy cliffs, ghosts of dust's past kicking up all around you. I see you climb and climb and climb. I see the peak of the canyon grow further from your shaky grasp. I see you transfix. I see you call out for somebody, for anybody. But I can't hear you. I can't help you. My legs go quicksand.

I'm spellbound and miniscule in this yawning crater, subsumed by the land. I'm 8 years removed from the Housatonic Valley. I wake up in tomorrow and see you inside of me. Your body, a seed in the wind, traipsing like a whisper in the hollow belly of the earth, still running after death from the soil's absorption.

OTHERLIFE

Do you ever wake up in a dream, as if you're not still asleep? And you look down at your body, but it's just a million weaving vines tangled to make the shape of you? And in that moment, there's blue between your thighs, you're naked like a book, and the vines feel more like your body than your body ever did? Are you afraid of that garden?

EPILOGUE

A POINT OF BALANCE BETWEEN TWO STARS

Table setting and silverware placement don't belong in the lexicon of my body, and neither does the word lexicon. I don't know the importance of granite countertops, and I've always wanted a wood floor. I learned all the fancy things I know from Amelia Bedelia books—like what it means to draw drapes or dress turkeys. Until I was 18, I got my hair cut in my mom's friend's basement on East Village, the same road where my dad's mechanic operated illegally out of his personal garage, before he died in a motorcycle accident. I know how to make my own Windex, how to cook gallons of red sauce from scratch for less than 5 bucks, how to tell if a cold Coors Light is actually cold enough. When she was still alive, my granny thought jumpsuits were sophisticated, so she bought me a powder blue mini jumpsuit at 6 years old. I loved playing pretend with her. I met heroin death in a classmate 4 years later. I can open a beer with my teeth, light a joint with a hot knife, triangulate the best spots to smoke in the Valley woods (#1 being the wells, under the deer trap, just past my house). I never knew what "new car smell" really was until a couple years ago. I love the BBQ shack run out of a trailer right off Rt. 34, overlooking the Housatonic River. My grandpa sucked the green out of lobsters—I always admired him for that. I might be able to show you how to split firewood on a stump, how to season it just right. My bedroom in my parents' home didn't have a door for over 10 years. Just a curtain. Sometimes I forget that my brother's '91 Camry doubled as an ashtray. When I got to college, I drank every night for three weeks because I forgot I liked learning and I didn't know anyone like me. I hated my excitement. Now, I think a lot about my friends stuck at home, practicing escapism and love with a Ouija board. This is the womb that I came from, the wild acid spitting in my chest. Sometimes I wonder if it's too late for me, as I drown in white wine, read poetry, and talk about math my parents never learned. So, I still search for the axis: the equation to calculate the balance between these two stars.

ACKNOWLEDGMENTS

Thank you to all my early readers—my partner, my dear friends who received my poems by text message late at night, my fellow workshoppers at Tulane & Miami who gave me community, my professors who provided me a space to create, my students, and everyone else who supported me to construct this work, piece by piece. I want to extend special gratitude for the journals and presses that believed in this work before it was whole:

"To My Granny," *The Book of Life After Death: Essays & Poems, Tolsun Books,* 2023
"The Dirt Which Births Us," and "I'm Getting There," *GASHER Journal,* 2021
"When I Was Four," *The Boiler Journal,* 2020
"I Was Born," *Leveler Poetry,* 2019
"A Point of Balance Between Two Stars," *Scalawag Magazine,* 2019
"Small Angry Mama," *The Cardiff Review,* 2019
"White Noise," *Wildness,* 2018
"Locust Bride" *Lotus-Eater Magazine,* 2017

NOTES

This book and the characters who appear in it are inspired by my family's history and my life. Even so, the collection remains speculative in nature and aims to understand the process of how a family can be deconstructed and reconstructed over time.

My father, Edward Holler Jr. (or Eddie) helped me write many of the poems in this manuscript by allowing me to interview him throughout 2018 and 2019. Lines that he directly phrased appear in the following poems: "An Only Moon," "Method Acting," "In Orbit," "Make Do," and "Boogie Down, St. Rose." I consider him a co-conspirator of this book and an essential part of the complicated mechanism that I call family.

The titles of "You Are Giving Me Some Other Love," and "If I Never See the Setting Sun Again," are both taken from songs by the "lost" soul band Penny and the Quarters.

"I'm In Florida With You," was written after James Fenton's poem, "I'm In Paris With You."

The title of, "I Still Smell You, Distance Aside" is taken from the lyrics in the song "Rain Smell" by Baths.

"When I Was Four" borrows a line from Tory Dent's poem, "The Murder of Beauty / The Beauty of Murder."

Lines from "Cannibal Flower" were written using rearranged language from Safiya Sinclair's book, *Cannibal*.

"Locust Bride" was written using a repurposed line from Kaveh Akbar's poem, "Being In This World Makes Me Feel Like a Time Traveler."

The title of "A Point of Balance Between Two Stars" comes from a line of Joy Harjo's poetry in the book *Secrets From The Center of the World*.

Maeve Holler is a writer, editor, poet, and educator. Her work has been published by *Tolsun Books, The Boiler Journal, Leveler, Scalawag Magazine, The Cardiff Review, Wildness,* and elsewhere. She is the recipient of the 2020 Alfred Boas Poetry Prize and was most recently nominated for a 2022 Pushcart Prize. Maeve holds an MFA in Creative Writing from the University of Miami and a BA in English & Gender and Sexuality Studies from Tulane University. She currently lives in New Orleans, Louisiana.

www.ingramcontent.com/pod-product-compliance
Lightning Source LLC
Chambersburg PA
CBHW020338170426
43200CB00006B/431